Killer Music

LISA EISENBERG

JOHN M
Lon

Laura Brewster Books

House of Laughs
Killer Music
Tiger Rose
Fast-Food King
Falling Star
Golden Idol

Editorial director: Robert G. Bander

Cover: Bob Haydock

Interior art: Karl Lichtenstein

Copyright © 1980 by Pitman Learning, Inc.
This edition © 1980 by Jonn Murray (Publishers) Ltd

Printed in the United States of America
ISBN 0-7195-3815-7

Contents

Chapter 1

Stolen Songs

Wingate Theatre, New York, 8:00 p.m.

Bright lights flashed and turned. Thick white smoke came from cakes of dry ice along the aisles. Blue grey smoke floated up from large iron pots. Black and white pictures of the moon hung from every wall. Gold and silver moons, stars, and suns hung from the ceiling. An old movie played on the back wall. Loud drumbeats pounded from behind the stage.

Suddenly everything grew still. The noise of the drums stopped. The last bits of smoke floated up towards the ceiling. The New York crowd sat up in their chairs.

Then the stage was filled with a bright, white light. Slowly two big, coloured stars that hung above the stage moved down from the ceiling. The five points of the stars were silver. The centres were deep red gold wheels. The wheels turned as the stars moved down. They turned so fast that they seemed to be on fire.

There wasn't a sound as Roddy Moon walked out under the giant stars. The gold handle of his guitar flashed under the light. His silver clothes shone. For a few seconds, he looked out at the crowd. The stars came to a stop. Roddy threw back his long, curly hair. And then he started to sing.

All at once, the room was filled with noise again. The people in the crowd were on their feet. They screamed, "Moon! Roddy Moon!"

The screaming lasted for several minutes. But at last the people grew still. They sat down, and Roddy Moon started the song again. The notes from his guitar were loud and strong.

As Roddy sang, the crowd's eyes were fixed on him. No one looked away. So no one saw the figure in the last seat of the last row—the figure who stood up and slipped out of the room.

Behind Stage, 8:10 p.m.

The silver flashlight threw a beam of light down the dark passage. Then the light played slowly across the dressing room door. Black letters spelled out the name "Roddy Moon."

Without a sound, a key was fitted into the door's lock. A hand turned the key once to the right. Then the dressing room door opened without a sound.

Moonlight shone in through the window. The flashlight went out. The figure crossed to the desk in the corner and put down the silver flashlight. Another key opened the top drawer. Long fingers pulled out eight sheets of music.

The moonlight fell across the black notes on the pages. The figure looked down at the music. For a few seconds, the night was filled with the sound of soft humming. But all at once, there was a new sound. Footsteps were coming down the passage outside.

In three quick moves, the figure locked the drawer, opened the window, and climbed out. The long fingers still held the sheets of music. But the silver flashlight was still sitting on the desk.

Kennedy Airport, Three
Weeks Later, 4:00 p.m.

"Please put on your seat belts," the voice said. "We will be landing in New York soon."

Laura Brewster put down her *Rock Magazine* and found the two ends of her seat belt. As she closed the belt, she looked out of the window to her right. The plane was flying over the Hudson River.

"Put on your seat belt," a voice on her left said.

"I just did," Laura began. She turned her head towards the voice, but there was no one. Then she looked down at the cage on the seat next to her. There was a small, green parrot inside. "Put on your seat belt," the bird said again.

"Be still, Ringo," Laura said. She fished in the pocket of her old, red sweater. Out came three sunflower seeds. Laura handed two to the parrot. She bit into the last one herself. Then she picked up *Rock Magazine* again.

Laura turned to the story about the rock star, Roddy Moon. She was interested in him for several reasons. She was an investigator for the Atco Insurance Company. And she was going to New York because of Roddy Moon. Atco had sold life, business, and voice insurance to Moon. Atco also ran a check on the rock star every few years. The check was part of the work of the investigator's office.

All at once, Laura put down the magazine. She remembered the letter Roddy Moon had sent to Atco. It had come just as she was leaving to catch the plane. She had not had time to read it.

She reached in her pocket and took out the letter. Then she felt around in the pocket for the silver letter opener she always kept with her. It wasn't there. She checked both pockets of her jeans. Then she looked around on her seat. At last she turned towards Ringo's cage.

Ringo had pulled the sharp letter opener into his cage. He was washing it off in his water dish.

Laura grabbed the opener from him. "Don't make me sorry I brought you," she said. She made a face as she thought of the trouble he had been already. She had had to make several calls to the airline manager just to get him on the plane. Then she had had to pay for two seats. And now the bird was stealing things from her pocket.

She shook her head and turned back to Roddy Moon's letter. She opened it and started to read. Moon wrote that someone was stealing songs he had written. The thief had sent Moon a note. It said Moon could buy the songs back—for a lot of money. Moon wanted Atco to help him find out who the thief was.

Laura hummed to herself for a few seconds. "Finding lost songs isn't really Atco's business," she thought out loud. "But it won't hurt to check it out."

She put the letter away. Then she opened *Rock Magazine* again. It showed a picture of Roddy Moon and his wife, Stella, singing with the group called The Sun. But the story said that Roddy had left the group. He had been singing on his own at the Wingate Theatre for three weeks. The crowds that came to see him were very big.

Laura looked at the picture of Stella Moon. The woman was tall, with long, black hair. The story said Stella was still singing with The Sun.

As Laura finished reading, the wheels of the plane touched down. When the plane came to a stop, she took off her seat belt and reached for her cap. Then she picked up Ringo's cage and her small bag and started for the door.

As she left the plane, she heard someone calling her name. She turned to see a red-haired woman coming up to her. The woman was about six feet tall. Laura guessed her weight at more than 200 pounds.

"Ms. Brewster? I'm Mag Chumbley," the woman said. "Mr. Moon's office sent me to pick you up. Come right this way."

"How did you know who I was?"

Mag gave a loud, deep laugh. "I didn't," she said. "I said 'Ms. Brewster' to every woman on the plane before I found you. You *don't* look much like an insurance investigator, you know."

Laura looked down at her old sweater and jeans and sighed. She thought, where have I heard *that* before? Then she followed the large woman out of the building. The air was cool. It felt like rain.

Mag went over to a long, black car. Laura opened the back door and climbed inside. She put Ringo's cage and her bag on the seat. Mag got in front and started the engine.

As they pulled out, a light rain started to fall. They drove for several miles without talking. Then Laura spoke. "Are we going to see Roddy Moon right away? Or can we go to the Dover Hotel first? I'd like to drop off my bird."

Mag acted as if she had not heard. She didn't even turn her head. Must be hard of hearing, Laura thought. That would fit with her loud voice. Laura sat forward on the seat. She was about to ask her question again. But then she looked down.

There was a gun on the front seat next to Mag's right hand.

CHAPTER 2

Roddy Moon's Problem

A Busy New York Street, The Same Day, 4:30 p.m.

Without speaking, Laura sat back in the seat. She thought about jumping out. But the car was going too fast.

She looked hard at the back of Mag's head. It would be easy to knock the woman out and grab the wheel. But she might not get to the wheel fast enough. The car might crash.

Finally Laura decided there was nothing she could do. She waited and looked out of the window. She wanted to remember the streets they were driving along.

Mag drove on for a few more miles. Then she came to a stop in front of an office building. The building was in a busy part of the city.

Laura saw Mag slip the gun into her pocket. Then the large woman climbed out of the car. She pulled open the back door and smiled. "Come on," she said. She pointed at the building. "We go right in here."

Slowly Laura turned to the door. As she did, she reached back and opened Ringo's cage. Then she stepped out of the car. She didn't close the door. She walked around in front of Mag.

The large woman took Laura's arm. "This way," she said. All at once, a green shape flew out of the car. Ringo screamed, "Put on your seat belt!" Then he landed on top of Mag's red hair.

Mag's mouth fell open. She let go of Laura's arm and grabbed at the bird. Laura turned and ran around the corner. With a rush of wings, Ringo flew after her.

Two blocks away, Laura flagged down a yellow taxi.

"Dover Hotel," she told the driver. "And hurry!"

The taxi pulled away. Laura turned to see if they were being followed. No one seemed to be watching them. What a great welcome, Laura thought. She sat back and waited for her heart to slow down. A few minutes later, the taxi came to a stop.

The Dover Hotel was in a small street in an older part of New York. A white-haired man dressed in blue stood by the door. He smiled at Laura as he held the door for her. He didn't seem surprised by Ringo on her arm.

Atco had booked a room for Laura, so her key was ready at the front desk. The woman at the desk told her how to get to room 201. Laura climbed the stairs to the room and locked herself and Ringo inside.

The room had white walls and a big, yellow bed. There was a round, blue chair in the corner. High windows looked out on a side street. "Too bad we won't be staying long, Ringo," Laura said. "A few nice plants and this could be home."

Laura looked out at the rain for a minute. Then she went to the telephone. She called the number she had been given for Roddy Moon.

She heard the telephone ring once. She hummed to herself as she waited. After 12 rings, she hung up.

Laura looked around. "Just what I need," she said. A New York map lay on a small table near the bed. She picked it up and found the Wingate Theatre, where Roddy was singing. It was only a few blocks from the Dover. Laura looked out of the window again and saw that the rain had stopped. She decided to walk.

Before she left, she gave Ringo some sunflower seeds and ate one herself. She pushed her curly hair away from her face and pulled on her cap. Then she opened the door and stepped out into the passage.

Suddenly, she found herself looking up at Mag's large face. The red-haired woman was holding Ringo's cage and Laura's bag. A small, thin man was standing beside her. He smiled at Laura.

"I'm Don Montez," he said. "Roddy Moon's business manager. And I understand you already know Mag."

"I know her, but I don't like her act," Laura said. "Why was she carrying a gun? And why wouldn't she tell me where we were going?"

"Mag is my bodyguard. I have a lot of business interests. So I have to be careful. Mag was bringing you to see me. She should have told you that. But she is under orders not to answer questions about me."

"Sorry," Mag said. She handed Laura Ringo's cage and the small bag. Laura got out her room key and opened the door again. She held it while Mag and Don Montez went inside.

The manager walked over to the yellow bed and sat down on it. Laura put down her things and went to the middle of the room. She asked, "Why did you want to see me?"

"I wanted to talk to you before you went to see Roddy," Montez said. "I think he has a problem."

"Like what?"

"I'm not sure. But he has been acting strange for a while. First he broke off with The Sun. And now he and his wife fight all the time. But he won't tell me why."

Laura laughed. "What's so strange about that? Maybe he won't talk about it because it isn't any of your business," she said.

"But Roddy Moon *is* my business," said Don Montez. "And I'm sure he has something on his mind. *You* can help me find out what it is."

Laura thought of the letter she had read on the plane. But she didn't say anything about it. "If there is something wrong with Roddy, Atco should know about it," Laura said. "He has a lot of insurance with us. But if I learn anything, I'll tell my company. Not you."

She got up and started for the door. "And now I'm going to see Roddy Moon," she said. "Maybe I'll catch you at his show tonight."

Don Montez and Mag followed Laura out of the Dover. They wanted to drive her to the Wingate Theatre. But Laura said she would rather walk.

By the time she got to the Wingate, it was raining hard. She pulled her sweater up around her neck. Then she started up the front steps. There was a big crowd there. They were all waiting to see Roddy Moon. They didn't seem to mind the rain.

Laura pushed her way through the people. She started towards the main door. A guard stopped her.

"Hold it," he said. "You'll have to wait with the others. The show isn't until tonight."

"I know," Laura began. "But—"

Before she could finish, the crowd had pushed her away from the door. She saw the guard go inside and close the door. Then she walked around to the side of the building.

She tried a side door, but it was locked. She went to the back of the building and found another door. It was locked, too. The rain was beating down on her head.

Laura looked around. No one was in sight. She put her hand into her sweater pocket and pulled out her silver letter opener. She started to pick the lock on the door.

Suddenly she felt a strong hand on her arm. An angry voice asked, "What do you think you're doing?"

CHAPTER 3

Rock Concert

Wingate Theatre, The Same Day, 6:00 p.m.

Laura slipped the letter opener back into her
pocket. She turned around. A heavy man was
holding her arm. Even through the rain, she
saw that his face was round and red. The man
looked angry.

The man asked his question again. "What do
you think you're doing?"

With her free hand, Laura reached into the
back pocket of her jeans. She pulled out her
Atco I.D. card. "I had some trouble getting in
the front," she said. "Roddy Moon knows I'm
coming."

The heavy man looked at the card. "This looks OK. I'll let you in. My name is Alf MacDougal," he said. "But you can call me Pops. Everyone does. I take care of things around here." He gave Laura her card. Then he reached for the ring of keys hanging from his belt. He opened the back door.

Laura followed Pops into the building. "I'll take you around to Mr. Moon's dressing room," Pops said. "We can cut right through the big room. This is where Mr. Moon does his show."

He opened the door to a large room with a stage. Then he led Laura down the centre aisle. "I used to be in show business once," Pops said. "I did everything. I told jokes and sang and danced. I had an act where I dressed up as ten different people. I'd come out as one person. Then I'd run inside a big black box. A few seconds later, I'd come out as someone else. I still have all my old disguises."

"I'd love to see them," Laura said.

Pops shook his head. "That's all part of the past," he said. "Now I clean up after the big rock shows they have in here. It's not a great job. And rock music is just a lot of noise to me. I hate the stuff."

He stepped up on the stage. Laura followed him. Then he stopped and looked up. "Another light is out up there," he said. "I'll have to climb up and fix it. I'm getting too old for this work. I'd rather be out on my farm."

He went over to a wooden ladder on the back wall near the door. It led up to rows of beams above the stage.

Laura asked, "Are those old beams safe?"

"Oh, yes," Pops answered. "I've checked them myself. They have to hold up those things for Mr. Moon's show." He pointed towards two large stars standing against the back wall. Laura gave one of the stars a small push.

"Pretty heavy," she said.

Pops touched the wheel in the centre of each star. "Each one of these has a motor," he said. "That's why the stars weigh so much." Then he opened a back door, pointing towards a dark passage. "The dressing room is right in there," he said. "Just knock on the door. I'm going to fix that stage light." He walked off talking to himself.

Laura went along the passage. She heard someone singing. Soon she found a door with "Roddy Moon" printed on it. The voice was coming from inside. Now Laura could make out the words. "I found you in the rain. Will I see you again?"

The notes were low and sad. Laura waited for the song to go on. But everything was still. At last she knocked on the dressing room door. A voice called for her to come in.

Roddy Moon was sitting behind a desk that was covered with sheets of music. He was holding a pen in one hand. He was wearing jeans and a shirt. His silver show clothes hung over the back of a chair.

"I'm Laura Brewster, the insurance investigator," Laura began. "My company wrote you that I was coming."

Roddy looked at her and smiled. "Can I talk to you later? I just got an idea for a new song. I want to write it down right away," he said. He pulled at a piece of his long, curly hair. "Why don't you come back here after the show?"

"OK," Laura said. She headed out of the door down the passage. Then she heard Roddy call her.

"Laura? Would you mind keeping something for me? Just until tonight?"

Laura came back to the dressing room door. "Don't give me anything worth a lot of money," she said.

Roddy laughed. "Nothing like that," he said. He held out his right hand. In it was a little silver flashlight. Laura took it and put it in the pocket of her sweater. When she looked up, Roddy had already turned back to his music. She went out of the door and back along the dark passage.

As she came around the corner, she ran into Pops. He was talking to himself as he put away some tools. When he saw Laura, he stopped. Then he led her to a seat just off the stage. "This is the best spot to see the act from," he said. "Now I have to get on with some more work." He turned and walked across the stage. "See you later," he called.

Laura waved to Pops. When he was gone, she left her seat and went to the centre of the stage. She looked out at the rows of seats. "I wonder what it's like to be a rock star," she said to herself. She danced around for a minute and then laughed. Pretty funny, she thought. Still laughing, she walked back to her seat and watched the people prepare for Roddy's show.

Half an hour later, the crowd started to come into the theatre. Laura stayed in her seat. She watched a very thin woman in a long, black dress walk to a seat in front of the stage. The woman's thick, yellow hair stood out all around her head. Her faced was painted dead white.

Laura touched her own short hair and smiled. Then she turned to look at a young man near the centre aisle. He was wearing nothing but a pair of old jeans. He had silver moons painted on his back, arms, and face. He was jumping up and down in a wild dance. As he danced, he sang one of Roddy Moon's songs.

A little while later, the room was full. Every seat was taken, and a lot of people were standing. They were crowded into the back of the room and around the foot of the stage.

Soon, lights on every side of the room started to flash on and off. The loud beat of drums filled the air. Smoke floated up through the room. Pictures of the moon and stars played on the walls. Large hanging glass balls turned around and around high above the stage. They caught flashing beams of light and shot them out at the crowd.

For the next few minutes, things in the room became more and more wild. The air grew grey with the smoke from the iron pots. The noise of heavy drumbeats crashed against the walls. The whole room seemed to move.

Then, all at once, the noise stopped and the lights went out. The people in the room grew very still.

Slowly the two giant stars came down from the ceiling. Their centre wheels looked like circles of fire. Their points flashed and shone.

Then the rock star walked onto the stage. The stars stopped just above him. With one hand, he held his gold-handled guitar. With the other, he waved.

The people went wild. Some jumped up and down. Others screamed and called out, "Moon! Moon!"

At last Roddy picked up his guitar with both hands. He started to sing "Dead Planets," his first big hit. As he sang, he held his guitar close to his body. His curly hair floated out around his head.

Laura loved the song. But she didn't look at Roddy as he sang. She watched one of the giant silver stars above him. At the start of the song, it had started to move. Now it was slowly swinging.

All at once, Roddy stopped singing. He looked up at the ceiling. A wild look came over his face.

Laura jumped to her feet. She started onto the stage towards Roddy. But suddenly two strong hands closed around her neck from behind. She kicked and tried to break away. Then she felt a sharp blow on the side of her head. She began to fall. And everything went black.

Chapter 4

Fear in the Subway

A Small Room, The Same Night, 9:00 p.m.

As Laura opened her eyes, her head was pounding. The inside of her mouth was very dry. Her whole body felt stiff.

She was on her side on a dirty wooden floor, and looking at a blank wall. Her hands were tied together in front of her. When she tried to move her feet, she found that they were tied too.

For a while, she lay still. Then she rolled over on her back. She saw that she was in a small room. A weak beam of light shone through a window above her.

Laura spent the next few minutes trying to work herself free. But the ropes were tied too well. At last, she gave up.

She rested for a few seconds. Then she used her feet to push herself towards the wall. She turned on her side again. Slowly she worked until she was sitting up with her back against the wall.

Now she could get her tied hands into her pocket. She felt for her letter opener and pulled it out. She took it between her fingers. She started to cut away the ropes around her feet.

Because her hands were tied, this work went very slowly. But at last, the rope was cut through. Laura sighed as she moved her feet. She was able to slide her back up along the wall. As she stood up, the room seemed to spin around.

She shook her head to clear it. Then she walked slowly across the room to the door. Her legs felt weak and stiff.

The door was locked. Laura started to pound on it and yell. Finally she heard the sound of footsteps outside the door.

"I'm locked in!" Laura called.

A woman answered. "I'll go get Pops," she said. And Laura knew she was still in the Wingate.

A few minutes later, a key turned in the lock. The door opened. Pops and a young woman came into the room. The woman had long, black hair. Laura had seen her picture in *Rock Magazine*. She was Roddy Moon's wife, Stella.

As Pops looked at Laura, his eyes grew wide. "What happened?" He started to take the ropes off her hands.

"I wish I knew," Laura answered. "What happened to Roddy?"

Stella and Pops looked at each other. Then Stella's large eyes filled with tears. "A star fell on him and—and killed him," she said. Then she turned and ran out.

Pops looked after her and shook his head. "She wanted Roddy to go back with The Sun," he said. "She didn't like singing without him. But I guess a life insurance cheque will make her feel better." He turned back to Laura, but she was still looking after Stella Moon. "Mr. Montez has been looking for you," Pops went on. "You can find him in Mr. Moon's dressing room. I'll take you back there."

Laura followed Pops down some dark stairs that led to the big room. A police officer was walking around on the stage. Pops stayed behind to talk to him. Laura went on by herself.

Don Montez was sitting behind the desk in Roddy's dressing room. His face looked sad. As Laura came in, he said, "You look sick. What happened to you?"

"I thought you might tell *me* what happened. You or Mag."

"Mag has the day off," the manager said. Then he shook his dark head. "What a strange accident," he said. "I'm still not sure how it could have happened."

"Just what *did* happen? Someone didn't want me to know." Laura made a face as she felt the bump on the side of her head.

"The wire that held one of the stars broke," the manager said. "The star fell and hit Roddy. He died from a blow to the head. Anyway, that's what everyone thinks. No one really saw what happened."

"What do you mean?"

"Just as the star came down, all the lights went out. There must have been a short in the wires or something. No one could see a thing."

Laura didn't say anything for a long minute. Her fingers beat a soft song on the desk. "The lights just *happened* to go out," she said. "Just at that second. Something sounds a little strange. But my head hurts too much to think." She turned towards the door. "I may want to talk to you later. And if you think of anything to tell me, I'll be at the Dover Hotel."

As she went into the hall, Don Montez followed her. "Your company is going to have to pay out a lot of insurance money," he said. "It's bad luck for them."

"It was worse luck for Roddy," said Laura. She walked down the passage and back through the big room. Then she opened the front door of the Wingate and stepped outside. She had never felt more tired. She knew she had to lie down and rest her head. She decided the Subway train would be the best way back to the Dover.

She took out her street map and looked at it. Then she started walking towards the nearest Subway station. Along the way, she found a shop that sold sunflower seeds. She bought two small bags and bit into a few seeds right away. Then she walked down the stairs to the Subway.

There was a small crowd of people waiting for a train. Laura went over and stood by a heavy man with long, white hair. Soon she heard a train coming. She moved forward with the rest of the people.

Just then, someone said, "That train doesn't stop at this station. It goes on through." The crowd moved back.

The train was speeding towards the station. Suddenly Laura felt someone standing very close behind her—too close. She took a step forward. The person moved up, too. They were only inches away from the track now.

Laura started to turn to say something. She didn't like being crowded that way. But all at once she felt a push. She started to fall forward. Right in front of the speeding train.

CHAPTER 5

A Visitor to New York

**Subway Train Station,
The Same Night, 9:30 p.m.**

"Watch it!" a voice called out. A hand grabbed Laura's arm and pulled her back. The train rushed past. Laura turned to see who had helped her. Once again, she was looking at Mag's large face.

"You should be more careful," Mag said with a little laugh. "You could get yourself killed that way."

Laura looked behind Mag, trying to see who had pushed her. Several people had moved away from the crowd. And she thought she saw a white-haired man rushing up the stairs to the street. I wonder what his hurry is, Laura thought. Why isn't he waiting for the next train?

"I'm starting to feel New York isn't a very safe place," Laura said. "By the way, I thought you had the day off."

"I did. But I came back when I heard about Roddy. I just got off the train that's standing over there. Just think of it—killed by one of his own stars!"

"How did you hear about it?"

"Oh, Mr. Montez called to tell me. And then I heard it on the radio. But you don't have time to talk, dear. Here comes your train." Mag waved good-bye and headed up the stairs towards the street.

As Laura got on the train, she looked at the people around her. No one seemed to be looking at her. She sat down and started to think. Someone wants me out of the way, she thought to herself. Maybe it was the heavy, white-haired man. But who is he?

Then she wondered why Mag had been in the same subway station. Maybe she followed me there. Maybe *she* pushed me, Laura thought.

Maybe she wants to frighten me away. Maybe she is afraid I'll find out something about how Roddy died. And *why* Roddy died. There are too many things just *happening* around here.

Three stops later, Laura was still in deep thought. She got off the train and walked the few blocks to the Dover. She walked into the hotel. The man in blue waved to her.

Slowly she climbed the stairs to room 201. She got her key out, opened the door, and went into the room. All I want to do is sleep, she thought.

Suddenly her heart stood still. The room was dark. But she could see someone sitting in the blue chair.

She stepped back into the passage. A voice called out to her. "I thought you would never get back," it said. "I've been here for an hour. Where have you been?"

Laura's mouth fell open. "I don't believe this," she said. She went inside and turned on the light. She looked at Police Lieutenant Luke Norton's long face and square chin. He stood up and smiled.

Laura's voice was angry as she said, "What are you doing here?" As she talked, Ringo flew to her arm and put his head in her pocket. He came out with a sunflower seed. "Didn't you think I could handle this job by myself? Do you still think you need to check up on me?"

Luke shook his head. "I got two weeks off," he said. "So I decided to take my vacation in New York. Why are you so angry? I thought we could have dinner together."

After a second, Laura smiled. "I'm sorry," she said. "I've been through a lot. And my head hurts. I—wait a minute. How did you get into my room?"

"The door was open. So I came in and made myself at home. I've been resting and talking to your parrot. He learned something new since the last time I saw him."

"I know—put on your seat belt!"

"No," said Luke with a laugh. "This is different. He keeps saying, 'Where could she have put it?' Have you lost something?"

"No," Laura said. Then her eyes grew wide. "Ringo says only what he hears. And he didn't hear that from me," she said. "Did you say the door was open when you got here?"

"Yes," said Luke. "In fact, the maid had just come out. She was carrying a pile of sheets."

"The *maid?* They told me they change the sheets in the morning here. What did she look like?"

"I didn't see her face. But she was pretty fat. I called hello to her. She had a low voice."

"If it wasn't a real maid, I wonder what she was looking for. And how she—or he—got the door open."

"That's easy," said Luke. "There's an old iron fire escape right outside your room. I saw it while I was waiting for you." He walked over to one of the windows and pushed it. It opened. "I'll see if I can find anything."

Luke put his head out of the window, then climbed out onto the iron stairs. He turned around to face Laura. He started to say something. Suddenly a shot rang out.

A strange look came over Luke's face. He took a step back. He grabbed his side. Then he sat down hard on the stairs.

Laura ran to the window and climbed out. She went to Luke's side. His eyes were closed. But he opened them when she touched his arm.

"Go after them," he told her. "They may still be near here."

"I can't leave you like this, Luke."

"I'm OK," he said. He put his hand over the blood on the side of his shirt. He tried to smile.

Laura gave him a quick look. She climbed back in the window. She telephoned the front desk for help. Then she went back to the fire escape.

"A doctor is on the way, Luke," she said. "I'm going after the person who shot you. You'll be OK here. I don't think anyone meant to shoot you at all. In the dark, they probably thought you were me. Someone has been trying to kill me all night."

Without looking back, Laura started down the fire escape. Luke didn't say anything at all. His head was resting on an iron step. He had passed out.

CHAPTER 6

The Wig
and Pen

**The Streets of New York,
The Same Night, 10:00 p.m.**

As Laura came down the stairs, she heard someone running. She tried to head towards the sound. But she wasn't sure where it came from.

She started to run up and down the streets near the Dover. Soon it started to rain again. Laura felt her wet hair and wished she had her cap with her. But she kept going. She ran as long as she could stand it. Then she slowed down to a walk. Once she spotted a dark figure turning a corner. But seconds later, when she got to the corner, no one was there.

At last she decided to give up. She was very wet and tired. She turned around and headed back the way she had come.

When she got to the Dover, she checked with the front desk. There were two notes for her. One said that Luke had been taken to City Hospital. The other said that Stella Moon had called twice. She wanted to meet Laura at 11:00 at a place called the Wig and Pen.

Laura climbed the stairs to room 201 and went inside. She wanted to dry off before going to see how Luke was. She took off her wet sweater and threw it over the back of the blue chair. Just then, she saw Luke Norton's black coat on the bed. She grabbed it and put it on.

"It doesn't fit," she said to Ringo. "But it should keep me dry." She found her cap and pulled it on, too.

The coat was very long. As Laura walked down the stairs, she almost tripped over it. She tried to hold it up as she went outside. The man in blue was in front of the hotel. Laura asked him about the Wig and Pen.

A strange look came over the man's face. "It's by the river," he said. "But it's not a very nice place."

"I'll be careful," Laura said. Then she asked him where she could get something quick to eat. The man pointed her to a hamburger stand on the corner. Laura went there and ate two hamburgers. Then she hailed a taxi.

When she got to City Hospital, she met a Dr. Wallingford in the hall. He wouldn't let her go into Luke's room.

"The shot went right through his side," the doctor said. "He's very weak."

"But will he be all right?"

Dr. Wallingford smiled. "You can see him tomorrow," he said. "And ask him for yourself. But I'd say everything will be OK."

Laura thanked the doctor. Then she went down the stairs and out to the street. She hailed another taxi. She told the driver to go to the Wig and Pen. As she climbed into the back seat, she pulled Luke's long coat around her. I guess I have a few seconds to think, she smiled to herself. I don't get many of those. She thought about the reasons people had for killing Roddy.

Stella Moon had two reasons. She had been angry at Roddy because he had left The Sun. And she would get a lot of insurance money because he had died. Don Montez would get some insurance money, too. And Mag would do anything Don Montez told her to do.

As the taxi turned south, Laura thought about the man down in the Subway station. And she wondered about the maid in the Dover. Who were they? How did they fit in?

The taxi drove past several dark city blocks. Then it headed down a street that ran along the Hudson River. After a while, the driver stopped in front of a small, dirty building.

"This is it, Miss," the driver said. "Are you sure you want to get out here?"

Laura handed him some money and opened her door. "I'm sure," she said. "Thanks."

As she watched the taxi drive away, she could smell the river behind her. She looked up and down the street once. Then she walked into the Wig and Pen.

The inside of the building was very dark. Only a few people were there. They didn't even seem to see Laura.

At last Laura made out Stella Moon's dark head in the corner. She went over to her and sat down. Stella had not touched the food in front of her.

"I'm sorry to make you come here," Stella said. "It's a pretty bad place. But I didn't want anyone to see us together."

"That's all right. What did you want to see me about?"

"It's about Roddy. I know what people are saying. And it's true that he and I were fighting. I wanted him to stay with The Sun. But . . . ."

"But what?"

Stella sat forward in her chair. "But I didn't want him *dead* because of it."

Laura drummed her fingers on the table. "Where were you when the star fell on Roddy?"

Stella took a quick look around the room. When she answered, her voice was very low. "I was out in front watching the show. But I know who caused the star to fall on him. And why."

CHAPTER 7

Laura Followed

The Wig and Pen, The Same Night, 11:00 p.m.

Laura sat very still. "Are you sure, Stella? If you know who did it, you should go to the police."

But Stella wasn't listening. She was watching a man coming towards her. Her eyes were wide and frightened. She looked ready to spring from her chair.

The man came close and put his face near Stella's. "You're Stella Moon! The rock star. Right?" He turned around and called to some of his friends. "Mack! Donny! Guess who is sitting over here!"

Stella pushed her chair away from the table. "You're thinking of someone else," she told the man. Then she crossed the room towards the door. Laura stood up and went after her.

When they got outside, Laura said, "We can't stay out here, Stella. This street is real trouble."

"Let me just tell you what I know," said Stella. "And I'll be done with it. Once and for all. Someone stole some songs from Roddy. But the person dropped something in Roddy's room. Roddy figured out who did it. And I heard him fighting with the person."

"You know who it was?"

"Yes," Stella began. Suddenly something moved behind her. Laura reached out to pull Stella away. But she was too late. A figure jumped forward out of the night. A long, dark arm went up and crashed down on Stella's head. The woman fell to the street.

It was too dark to tell who the figure was. But Laura saw it coming towards her, and she stepped back. Then she turned around and ran down the street.

Laura's feet hurt as they pounded against the hard stones of the street. The folds of

Luke's coat caught at her legs. She heard footsteps behind her. She looked for a place to hide. But there were no openings between the buildings that lined one side of the street.

At last, Laura saw a small side street. She turned down it. She ran hard. But she could still hear the footsteps at her back.

The little street was full of papers, bottles, and pieces of wood. Suddenly Laura's foot kicked a bottle. She heard it crash into a wall and break. Then a large rat ran in front of her, within inches of her feet. A strong, bad smell filled her nose.

All at once, it started to rain hard. Soon Laura could not see where she was going. She ran with both hands out in front of her. And still the footsteps splashed along behind her.

Suddenly Laura's hands touched something cold and hard. She came to a quick stop. She had almost bumped an iron railing. It went across the end of the little street.

She looked up, trying to see the top of the railing. It seemed to be very high. She thought she saw sharp, iron points along the top. But there was nothing else to do. She started to climb up.

The footsteps were very close now. Laura looked back and saw the figure moving through the rain.

With one hand, she grabbed the iron railing. She hung several feet above the street. As the figure came close, she let herself swing to the side. There was a loud crash as the figure smashed into the railing.

Laura hit the ground at a run. She raced back the way she had come. As she ran, she kicked more bottles and cans. Mud splashed all around her.

At last, she turned into the street by the river. She headed back towards the Wig and Pen. There had been a few people there. Maybe they would help her. Or let her use the telephone.

Before long, Laura's head started to hurt again. She felt tired and weak. She worked hard to keep her feet moving.

All at once, she knew that something had changed. The footsteps behind her were gone. She slowed down and looked back. No one was there. Then she saw the lights of a small car moving towards her.

"Maybe the car frightened the person away," she said to herself. She stood by the side of the street. She waved at the little white car as it came near her. A hand reached out of the window. It was holding a gun.

As Laura ducked away, two quick shots were fired. She threw herself against the side of a building. Two more shots hit the wall behind her head.

That's four, Laura thought. I hope there are only six shots in that gun.

Laura took off down the street again. She tried to get a look at the driver as the car pulled up beside her. But all she saw was a round face with a full, black beard. Then the hand reached out of the window again. Two more shots rang out in the wet night.

Laura watched the car slow down and turn around. Then it moved towards her again. She headed down the street the other way. The driver accelerated and came after her.

She threw herself to one side of the street. The car tried to pin her to a wall. Just in time, she ducked away. And no shots were fired.

Laura ran to the other side of the street. The car backed up, stopped, and came towards her. It picked up speed as it came.

Then Laura's foot hit a large piece of broken stone on the street. She fell down hard. The car seemed to move even faster. Laura pulled herself up. But Luke's coat slowed her down. And she was on the wrong side of the street. The side near the river.

The car raced forward. Laura turned and saw its two bright lights on her left. Suddenly the car made a sharp turn and just caught Laura's arm. Her feet left the ground.

She reached out for something to hold on to. Her fingers grabbed at empty air.

Laura fell for what seemed like a long time. Then she felt the cold, dark water of the river close over her head.

CHAPTER 8

The Missing Flashlight

On the River, The Same Night, 11:45 p.m.

When Laura woke up, she wasn't sure where she was. Her left arm hurt a lot. Her whole body felt cold. She reached up and touched her hair. It was wet and sticking to her face. Her cap was gone. Well, she thought. I hope my cap is all I lost!

Everything around Laura smelled of fish. And she thought she heard an engine.

"Bessie!" Laura heard a voice call out. "Bessie! She woke up!"

Laura turned her head. She saw two clear, blue eyes looking down at her. The eyes were warm and kind. Laura said, "Who are you?"

"I'm Rog," the man with the blue eyes answered. He pointed to his right. "And that's Bessie over there." The woman named Bessie looked around and waved at Laura. "You're on board our boat—the *Blue Bessie*," Rog went on. "We were coming up the river a while ago. Then we saw you. You were floating on the water. Your coat had caught on a post. We pulled you out. But I'm afraid we lost the coat!"

"That coat was nothing but trouble," Laura laughed. "Thanks for your help." She tried to sit up.

Rog pushed her back down. "You take it easy, Miss," he said. "You have a big bump on your head. You should rest. I can't guess why you were swimming in the Hudson. It's a pretty dirty river."

Laura smiled and closed her eyes. Then she heard Rog move away. She thought, the only time I get to think on this job is before and after accidents.

Then, in her mind, Laura went over each step she had taken in New York. The trouble started with Mag, she thought. Then, there was more trouble as soon as I talked to Roddy.

That's when everyone started trying to kill me. But Roddy didn't tell me anything. Then Laura opened her eyes. He didn't tell me anything, but he did *give* me something—the flashlight! That must be what Stella was talking about—the thing someone dropped in Roddy's dressing room. Roddy must have figured out who the flashlight belongs to. Laura tried to remember where the flashlight was. She thought she had left it in her sweater pocket. And the sweater was back in her room at the Dover. The room someone had broken into.

There was no question now in Laura's mind that someone had killed Roddy. That someone must have done something to the wire that held the star over Roddy's head. Then he or she had shorted the lights. And in the dark, the person could have gone out on the stage to make sure Roddy was dead. And maybe even hit him again.

"But before the lights went out, the person knocked me out," Laura said out loud. "I was the only one close enough to help Roddy."

Slowly Laura sat up. She knew she had figured a few things out. But she still didn't know the most important answers. Who killed Roddy? And who were all the people trying to kill her?

In a few minutes, *Blue Bessie's* engine cut out. Bessie and Rog steered the boat in and tied it to the jetty. Rog wanted to take Laura to City Hospital. But she said she was all right. She thanked the couple and shook their hands.

Then she went back up to the wet street. She flagged down a taxi. As she rode, she lay down on the seat. The driver woke her up when they came to the Dover.

When Laura turned on the light in her room, she saw her sweater. It was on the blue chair, where she had left it. Ringo was sitting next to it. He was eating a sunflower seed.

Laura walked over to the sweater. She went through both pockets. In one was half a bag of seeds. The other pocket was empty. The little silver flashlight was gone.

Just then, Ringo finished his seed. Slowly he walked along the back of the chair. He put his head into the pocket of the sweater. His green and red tail pointed up in the air. In two seconds, he came back out of the pocket. He held a big sunflower seed in his mouth.

Laura watched Ringo while humming a little song to herself. She drummed her fingers on the bed. Then she got up and went over to Ringo's cage.

Laura smiled. Her silver letter opener was sticking out of the parrot's water dish. The little silver flashlight was right next to it. Laura reached into the cage and pulled them out. She sat down on the blue chair to look at the flashlight. Ringo climbed onto her arm. He started to pick at her shirt.

"Thanks a lot, you silly bird," Laura said to him. "I was about to start worrying about this flashlight."

She turned the flashlight over in her hand. There was a letter *M* printed on the bottom. Laura ran her finger over it. Then she slipped the flashlight into her pocket.

Next she went to the telephone and called City Hospital. The nurse she talked to said Stella Moon had been brought in and would be all right. Then Laura asked to speak to Luke Norton. She was told that he was sleeping. Laura thanked the nurse and hung up.

Then she went back out into the wet New York night.

CHAPTER 9

Ringo Talks

**Wingate Theatre, Early the Next
Morning, 12:30 a.m.**

By the time Laura got to the Wingate, the
rain had stopped. The moon was high in the
sky. Laura started to pick the lock on the side
door. But she found the door was already open.

She stepped inside and turned on the silver
flashlight. Then she went slowly down the long
passage. Soon she reached the room where
Roddy had died. She climbed onto the stage.
As she started to look around, she thought she
heard guitar music. She stood very still and
listened.

It *was* music. Laura moved toward the back of the stage. She opened the side door. The guitar music was very loud. It seemed to be coming from Roddy's dressing room.

Slowly Laura moved into the passage. Then she stood still again. There was no sound in the building. The music had stopped.

Laura went down the passage. She turned off the flashlight when she came to Roddy's dressing room. She put it in her pocket and opened the door. The light of the moon shone in through the window. Laura could see Roddy's guitar on the desk.

She went over and touched the gold handle. It was warm, as if someone had just been holding it. She ran her fingers over the guitar's strings. They made a soft noise.

Suddenly the dressing room was filled with light. Laura wheeled around. A face was looking at her around the door. Laura's blood ran cold. The face was Roddy Moon's!

For a long minute, Laura didn't move. She could not take her eyes off the circle of bright, curly hair. Then the "ghost" with Roddy's face spoke.

"I knew you would come," it said. "All I had to do was wait."

At last, Laura found her voice. "I know who you are," she said. "And I know you killed Roddy."

The ghost stepped into the room. Its silver clothes flashed in the light. It asked, "How did you figure it out?"

"My bird told me. You talk to yourself too much."

"I suppose you know *why* I did it?"

"Roddy found out you were stealing his songs. You left something that he knew was yours in his dressing room."

The ghost in silver moved forward. "That's right," it said. "My silver flashlight. Give it to me now."

As they talked, Laura looked around for a way to escape. She moved close to the desk.

"I knew you were trouble from the start," the figure went on. "I've been trying to get to you for hours. But this time you can't get away."

Laura looked down. Now there was a gun in the ghost's hand. She had seen that hand and gun before. In the car by the river.

As fast as she could, Laura turned around. With both hands, she grabbed the handle of the guitar. She picked it up and sent it swinging through the air. The guitar hit the figure and knocked it back against the wall.

Laura raced out the door. She ran down the dark passage through another door. She was back on the stage in the big room. She crossed the stage and jumped down into the centre aisle. She went up to the main door. It was locked.

Right then, Laura heard the ghost at the side door to the stage. It jumped down and started up the centre aisle towards her. Laura slipped along the side of the room, back to the stage. She circled around to the side door. But now it was locked, too. She was trapped.

In a few seconds, she heard footsteps coming back down the aisle. She felt along the wall behind the stage. Her hands touched the ladder that led up to the beams above. She started climbing. At last, she reached the top. Slowly she walked out onto one of the beams.

All at once, the whole room changed. Glass balls that hung from the ceiling high above started flashing and turning. Bright circles of gold and silver shot high across the stage. The figure had turned on the ceiling lights for the Roddy Moon show.

Suddenly a shot hit the wood near Laura's feet. She almost stepped off the beam. She rocked from side to side. Her arms waved in the air. Then she started to fall.

She caught the beam as she went down. She pulled herself back up and lay flat. Her heart was pounding.

With those lights on, this is the worst place to be, she thought. She kept her body flat. She inched her way back to the ladder. Slowly she started to climb back down.

When she was six feet from the floor, she stopped. She looked around for the ghost. It was darker near the floor, and she couldn't see the figure. But she did see a flash of silver near her right hand. She moved her fingers along the back wall. Suddenly they touched one of the giant hanging stars from Roddy's act.

Slowly Laura turned herself around on the ladder. She slipped both hands behind the heavy star. She started to call out a name again and again. She waited. Then she called again.

Then she saw the ghost come towards her. When the silver figure was close, she pushed hard against the star. As it fell forward, it caught the figure on the arm. The ghost fell back on the stage. The star crashed down on top of it.

Laura jumped off the ladder. She ran forward. As she got to the body, she pulled out the silver flashlight and turned it on. Then she reached out her hand and pulled hard. The Roddy Moon disguise came away in her fingers. The beam of the flashlight shone down on a round, heavy, red face.

Laura looked down and shook her head. Then she picked up the gun from where it lay on the floor. She started to push away the heavy star. "Come on, Pops," she said at last. "The show is over."

City Hospital, That Night, 8:30 p.m.

Loud music filled the small room. Stella Moon sang one last long, high note. The song ended with a crashing drumbeat. And then the crowd went wild.

Laura got up and turned off the television. She smiled over at Luke. He was still in his bed at City Hospital.

"It looks like The Sun is going to make it big," she said. "Even without Roddy Moon."

"I guess so," Luke said. "But how did Stella get out of here before I did?"

"She only got hit on the head. *You* were shot."

"Tell me something. Did you *know* before you caught him that it was Pops who killed Roddy? The *M* on the flashlight could have stood for anyone — Montez, Moon, MacDougal. Or even Mag!"

"I was pretty sure it was Pops," Laura said. "Because Ringo said, 'Where could she have put it?' That had to mean someone was in my room talking to himself. And I heard Pops do that a few times. Besides, he had keys to everything in the Wingate. So he could get at the music in Roddy's desk. *And* he was up on those beams above the stage all the time. So he could do something to the wire that held up the star. But. . . ."

"But what?"

"But I could *not* figure out who all the people were who were trying to kill me. The man with white hair, the fat maid, the bearded driver. If they were after me, one of them had probably killed Roddy. It wasn't until I saw someone disguised as Roddy that I remembered."

"Remembered what?"

"That Pops had told me he used to do a disguise act. After that, it all fitted together."

"But why did he steal the songs in the first place?"

"He needed the money to keep his farm," said Laura. "Besides, he never liked Roddy. And he *hated* rock music."

"He didn't like you much either," said Luke.

Laura laughed. "You can say that again!"

Then Luke ran a hand over his hair. "Listen, Laura," he began. "I get out of here tomorrow. And I still have some vacation time left. I thought we could visit New York together. You know, go to plays. Eat out. See the sights."

Laura shook her head. "Didn't I tell you? I have to go home tonight. The Atco office called today. They have a big job waiting for me. My plane leaves in an hour."

Luke's face fell. But then he smiled. "Just my luck. Well, have a good trip home."

"Thanks," said Laura. "Maybe I'll see you on my next job."

Then Laura turned towards the door. She went into the passage and picked up Ringo's cage. Humming to herself, she left City Hospital. As she hailed a taxi, she was already wondering what her next job would be.